Exploring TIME

Gillian Chapman
& Pam Robson

SIMON & SCHUSTER
YOUNG BOOKS

"Time is nature's way of keeping everything
from happening at once."

Anonymous

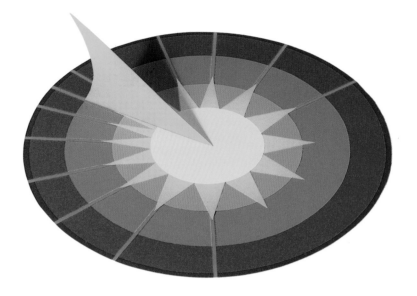

Special thanks to the following who lent items for the illustrations on pages 4, 5, 8 and 31
Brian Nelson, James Stirling & Tony
from Allsorts Model Shop,
Jean & John Flynn, Rupert Horrox and Keith Chapman

This book was prepared for
Simon & Schuster Young Books by
Globe Education of Nantwich, Cheshire

Visualisation and design: Gillian Chapman
Photography: Rupert Horrox

Additional photographs:
Ecoscene 16
Heather Angel 17

First published in 1994
by Simon & Schuster Young Books
Campus 400
Maylands Avenue
Hemel Hempstead, Herts HP2 7EZ

Text © 1994 Gillian Chapman & Pam Robson
Illustration © 1994 Gillian Chapman

A catalogue record for this book is available
from the British Library

ISBN 0-7500-1475-X

Printed and bound in Hong Kong
by Wing King Tong Ltd

Contents

Once Upon a Time...

Fiction

'Once upon a time...' is the familiar opening sentence to many well-known fairy stories. Such stories are about make-believe places and imaginary people. When you read a story you begin at the beginning and read on to the end—often the most exciting part.

Fact

True stories, about things that really happened in the past, are fact and are known as history. Events in history are usually described in the order in which they happened, that is in **chronological order.** One big difference between history and make-believe is that there is no real ending—events simply change with time. Time is a never ending journey in which past, present and future are all links in the same chain.

Passing the Time

When you have no means of telling the time the passage of time can seem faster or slower than usual. When you are happy and busy time seems to go by quickly. If you are sad and bored time can seem endless. Sometimes elderly people remember the past as if it were yesterday.

Our daily activities are governed by the weather and the seasons. In winter when the evenings are dark, we spend more time playing indoors or watching TV. In summer when the days are warmer and longer, we will enjoy more outdoor activities. Holiday times are often associated with festivals, times for celebration and relaxation.

What is Old?

As time passes, new things begin to look old. How old is your favourite toy? Can you remember when it was first given to you? If you have had it for a very long time you may not remember. Toys that have been played with a lot become scratched and worn, they may even have broken parts. As time passes, new toys become old toys.

My Time

Timing

Time is very important in all our lives. To be on time we use clocks and watches, otherwise we would miss the bus or be late for school. Sometimes we have **deadlines** to meet—an appointment to keep or a train to catch. We check the time on our watches and clocks many times a day. This helps us to **synchronise** our busy lives. **Punctuality** is being on time.

How do you spend your Time?

Think about a typical day—it could be a school day or a holiday. You expect to do certain things, like sleeping and eating, every day of your life. Other activities, like going to a club or watching a favourite programme on TV may only take place once a week. Can you imagine living through a whole day without knowing the time?

Put your Day in Order!

On strips of paper, write down 10 activities that you do every day. Jumble them up and ask a friend to arrange them in chronological order, that is in the correct order in which they happened. Do you clean your teeth before or after your breakfast? Think about what time it is when you carry out each activity. Mark the time on each strip.

get up	8.00
breakfast time	8.30
clean teeth	9.00
go shopping	10.30
lunchtime	12.30
play with friends	2.00
watch T.V.	4.30
suppertime	7.00
bath time	8.00
bed time	9.00

Time line for a Day

	Hours
Midnight	
Sleeping	8
Washing + Dressing	½
Breakfast	½
Shopping with parents	1½
Playing Sport	2½
Lunch	½
Playing with friends	2½
Teatime	½
Playing with friends	1½
Watching T.V.	½
Supper	½
Watching T.V.	1½
Washing + Dressing	½
Reading in bed	½
Sleeping	2½
Midnight	

Time Lines

A time line is a useful way to show events and happenings in chronological order. It can cover any length of time from a day to many millions of years. Make a time line showing how your time is spent. There are 24 hours in a day. Think about all the things you do in a day that take up your time. Use the information to calculate the amount of time spent on each activity. The total should be 24 hours. If it isn't then you have forgotten something.

Pie Charts

How you spend your day can also be explained on a pie chart. Divide the rim of a circle into 24 hours by first dividing it into 8 sections, then sub-dividing each section into 3 parts. Colour in the number of hours spent on each activity. You may be surprised to find how much time you spend in bed!

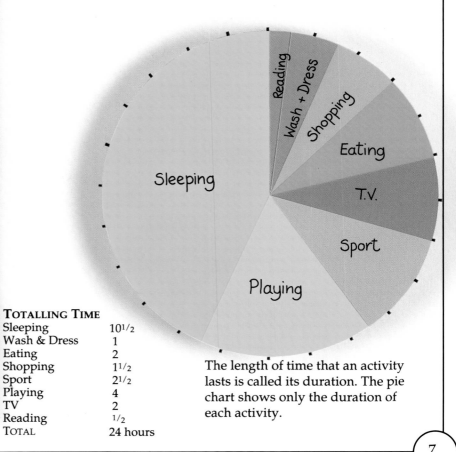

Totalling Time

Sleeping	10½
Wash & Dress	1
Eating	2
Shopping	1½
Sport	2½
Playing	4
TV	2
Reading	½
TOTAL	24 hours

The length of time that an activity lasts is called its duration. The pie chart shows only the duration of each activity.

Change over Time

Remembered Time
What do we mean by old? Most things change over time, some things take longer than others to become 'old'. An ancient mountain is a lot older than an old car. An old person is a lot older than your old toy.

Look at photographs of yourself when you were a baby. See how you have changed. Now look at photographs of your grandparents taken when they were very young. They have changed even more! Do you think your grandparents are old? What do we mean by an 'old' person?

Memories
People have their own memories to remind them of their childhood. They probably have scrap-books, photographs and diaries to look at. **Memorabilia** of this kind show how things change over time. Finding out about the past helps us to see that things do change as time passes. People make changes.

Keeping Records
Written evidence of the past is kept in **archives**. You can keep a personal historical record for yourself by writing a daily journal. Compile a family history and gather together old photographs to mount in an album.

MAKING A PHOTOGRAPH ALBUM
Look at your family's photograph albums and design an album of your own. Cut pages from dark paper, punch holes along one side and sew them together.

Natural Life spans

The life spans of plants and animals can last for just a few days or up to thousands of years. The study of their life stories is known as **natural history**.

Rate of Change

The natural world has ways of providing records. A tree's age is recorded inside the trunk. Each year that passes is marked in its structure. Observe the growth of a plant by taking careful measurements at the same time each week. Put the plant in a warm, light place and water the soil to keep it moist.

Rate of Growth

Record your findings in a growing book. Each week draw the plant at its correct height on paper of similar width. When it is fully grown sew the pages together to make a book. By recording the date you will establish the rate of growth. How long does it take for your plant to grow?

Keep a growth record of your own height and weight. Do you expect to grow every week, like the plant?

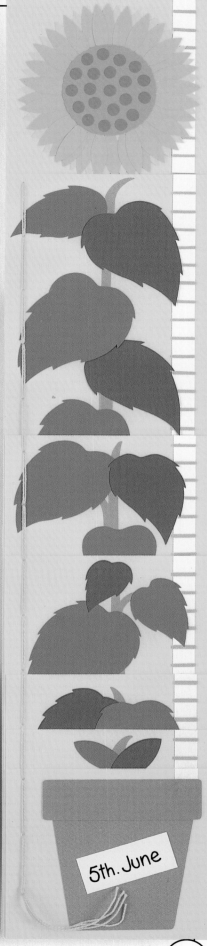

Sew the pages of the book together with a running stitch.

Planting and growing details can be recorded on the back of each page.

Mark the growth of the plant each week on the scale.

5th. June

12th. June

19th. June

5th. June

Lifetimes

Tracing your Ancestors

Anyone born before you is older than you. Who is the oldest living member of your family?

A **family tree** shows the births, marriages and deaths that have taken place in a family. If you wish to research your family, local records are kept in the registry office and parish register. Your oldest living relations will be able to help with information.

You may discover some interesting details about your **ancestors** which you could use to design a family crest.

Design your Family Tree

Your family tree will have you at the roots and different **generations** of your family on the branches. The further back in time you go, the higher up the tree you climb. Decide whether to follow either your mother's or father's family, it will be too complicated to put both on the same tree.

Design your family tree in an original way. You may have relations who are skilled at a sport or craft—think of ways to reflect this in your design. How can you show a death or divorce?

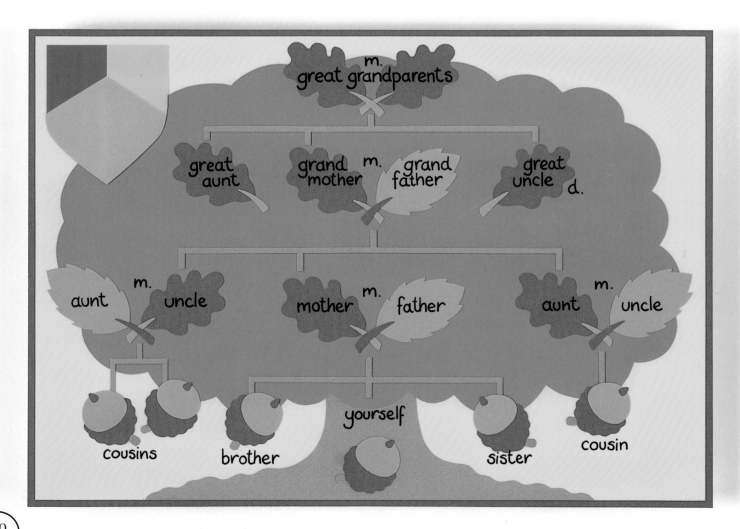

After two weeks the pupa splits open and the butterfly emerges.

Caterpillar spins a silken case around itself and hangs from the leaf. It changes into a pupa.

Eggs, laid on nettle leaves, take one week to hatch.

Caterpillar hatches from the egg and feeds off the leaf.

THE LIFE CYCLE OF A PEACOCK BUTTERFLY

Life Cycles

Plants and animals are all part of an energy cycle. The sun provides energy that plants use for growth. Some animals are herbivores that eat the plants. Others are carnivores that eat the herbivores. Dead animals and plants decay putting goodness into the soil to feed the plants once more.

A butterfly changes its form completely while developing. This process is called **metamorphosis**. Butterflies live for only a few months.

Toltec warriors, who lived in central America a thousand years ago, believed that if they died in battle they would have new lives as butterflies.

LIFE SPANS OF LIVING THINGS

Life Span

Every living thing has its own life span. The life span of a person can be a 100 years while parrots, tortoises and snakes can outlive people. Animals in a protected environment are likely to live longer than those in the wild. Mayflies appear on the same day, in the same place each year, then die two weeks later, but trees are the oldest living things on Earth.

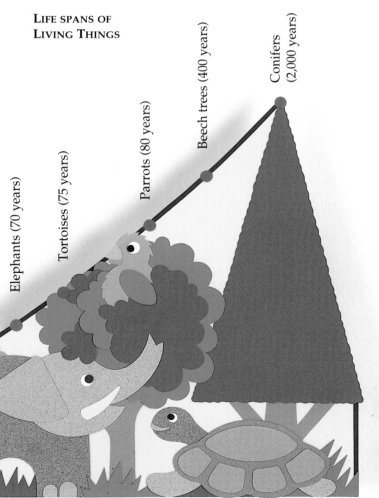

Germs (15–20 minutes)

Insects (3 weeks)

Sunflowers and slugs (1 year)

Dogs (12 years)

Pigs (15 years)

Silver birch (50 years)

Elephants (70 years)

Tortoises (75 years)

Parrots (80 years)

Beech trees (400 years)

Conifers (2,000 years)

Signalling Time

Waking Up!

Many people are woken in the morning by an alarm clock or a radio alarm. In the days before clocks were in general use, people relied on the sunrise to awaken them. Cocks crow at dawn and, in spring and early summer, most birds join the dawn chorus to lay claim each day to their territories.

NATURAL SIGNALS
In dry weather the scales of a fir cone open and the seeds fall out.

BEAN MAZE
Make a maze in a shoe box. Paint the inside of the box and the lid black. Punch a hole at one end.

Body Clocks

Living things have built-in biological clocks, geared to fit in with the natural rhythms of the environment—day and night, the solar year, the tides, the seasons. Patterns of behaviour are passed from parent to child, generation after generation. Birds, such as the cuckoo, know when the time has come to migrate. Creatures like the hedgehog, are ready to hibernate in late autumn.

People have body clocks that are governed by the cycle of day and night, this is called the **circadian rhythm**. The human cycle is about 25 hours, but we adapt to a 24 hour day. People who travel in aeroplanes across the world have to adjust quickly to new **time zones**. They often feel unwell because the natural rhythms of their bodies are upset by the time difference.

Plant a bean in a jar and stand it in the box at the opposite end to the hole. Put the lid back on the box and put it in a sunny place.

The bean shoots will grow around the maze towards the light coming through the hole.

All plants need light to grow. The shoots of the potato will be white. Chlorophyll, which makes them green, cannot do its job without sunlight.

Flower Clocks

Sunrise is the signal for many flowers to open. One of the first clocks was a flower border, planted with flowers that were known to open and close at certain times of day, following their own in-built clocks.

There is a flower so punctual that it is called the four o'clock flower— but it is poisonous, so be careful. The evening primrose opens at 6 p.m., the scarlet pimpernel closes at 2 p.m. In the Amazon forest a flowering cactus, called 'Queen of the Night' grows. It was first seen by the naturalist and artist, Margaret Mee, in 1981. It flowers each year, but only briefly after dark, then withers before dawn.

LIGHT SIGNALS
Seeds need moisture and warmth, but light is vital for them to grow properly.

Cut a round hole in a piece of cardboard and place it over the seeds.

Nocturnal Creatures

Bats sleep during the day. Nightfall is the signal for them to wake up to feed. Nocturnal creatures like badgers and owls also hunt their food at night.

Diurnal Creatures

Bees and butterflies are active during the day. They read the signals from the plants that tell them when nectar is being produced. Plants produce nectar at the same time each day.

Time to Grow

Most plants grow from seeds. A seed will not begin to grow unless the conditions are right—warmth and moisture signal **germination**. A few seeds need very special conditions before they will germinate. The cones of some pine trees need the very high temperatures caused by forest fires before they open to allow the seeds to fall to the ground. Seeds might wait 80 years for the signal to germinate.

Sow seeds, keep the soil moist and leave them in a sunny position.

See what happens when you prevent the seeds from getting the light they need.

Geological Time

History is concerned with true stories about peoples of the past but there are also stories of the Earth that have their beginnings millions of years before people existed. These stories are to be found as records in the Earth's rocks. The study of the history of these rocks is called **geology**.

Geologists can estimate the age of rocks by measuring small amounts of **radioactive** material caught inside when the rocks were formed. It is as though each different rock has its own precise clock.

The Earth is constantly changing but the changes happen very slowly so we cannot see them. The first person to grasp the idea of this continual change was Charles Darwin a scientist who lived in the 19th century.

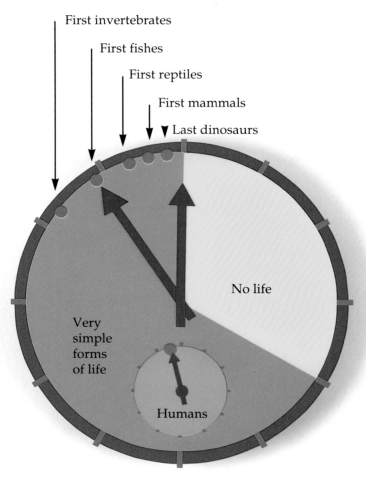

First invertebrates
First fishes
First reptiles
First mammals
Last dinosaurs
No life
Very simple forms of life
Humans

GEOLOGY CLOCK
The history of the Earth can be shown on a clock face. In the first 4 hours, there were no signs of life at all. During the next 7 hours, very simple life forms appeared. Fishes, dinosaurs and mammals were not seen until the last hour and human beings evolved only a few seconds before midnight.

SKELETON LEAVES
See if you can find some leaves in their final stages of decay. The 'skeletons' give you an good idea of what the fossil of a leaf looks like.

Pictures in the Rocks
The dead bodies of plants and animals are preserved in the rocks as **fossils** and show us what the ancient Earth was like. As the Earth changed, plants and animals changed in order to survive. This change is called evolution and it has been taking place continuously since the first living things appeared.

Running out of Time

On the geology 'clock' people appear at a minute to midnight. During that short time they have taken raw materials from the Earth that took millions of years to create and have used the planet as a rubbish tip. Many creatures have become extinct and more are threatened as people kill them, or destroy their habitat. Unless we learn to take better care of our planet, we could become extinct ourselves—just like the dinosaurs!

'Race Against Time'

Dinosaurs are an example of a species that did not survive, but there is plenty of evidence of their existence as fossils in the rocks. Play this game with a friend. Design a board like the one shown here. Which dinosaur is going to win the 'Race Against Time' by moving its eggs to a safe place?

RACE AGAINST TIME

Make a spinner, with twelve sections for the hours of the day. Use it like a die and spin a six to start moving each egg. Each player has 4 eggs, the winner is the first to move all its eggs to the safe cave.

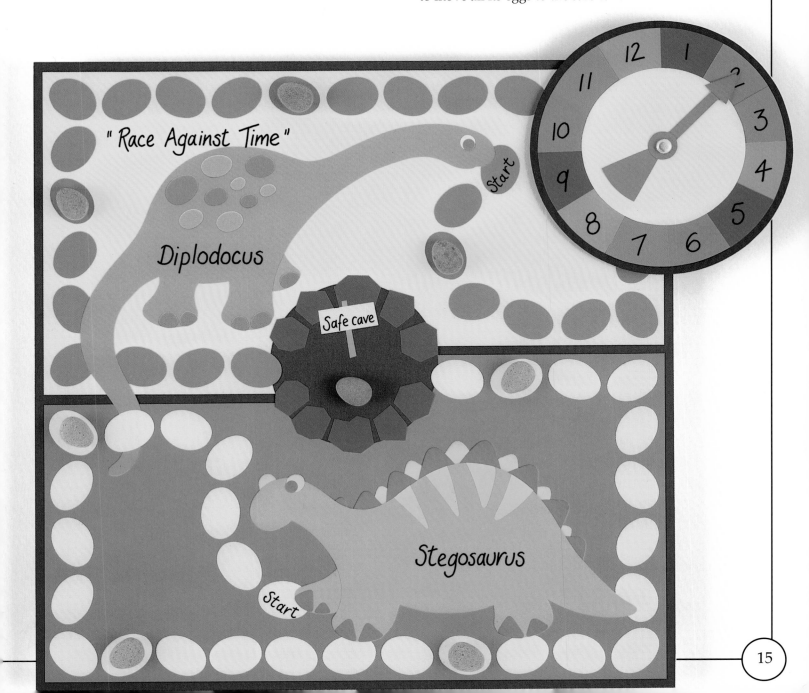

Historical Time

Looking back in Time
Things that happen today have become history by tomorrow. The natural world with its never-ending cycle of growth and decay provides a silent record. The oldest trees have lived through major events of the past. Bristlecone pines growing on the Rocky Mountains in the USA are the oldest living things on Earth.
Some were seedlings when the ancient Egyptians were building pyramids nearly 5,000 years ago in north Africa.

Recording the Years
The trunk of a felled tree is a little like a time machine—it can take us back through time. Each year the trunk becomes thicker as new wood grows. When the tree is cut down each year's growth can be seen as concentric rings. For a tree to reach maturity can take anything from 30 to 100 years.
A softwood, like a pine tree, generally grows faster than a hardwood tree, like mahogany.

Natural Log-books
Tree rings are a natural log-book. Sometimes their size and shape reveal interesting facts about the past. Dry weather means less growth, so it is possible to discover how the weather changed by examining the rings. Where they are close together shows a lack of rain. In North America, pine trees have scars left in the rings, evidence of forest fires that occurred every 13 years over a period of 256 years.

GROWTH RINGS
Cross-sections from very old trees, can have as many as 100 growth rings. If this tree was felled in 1945, it was probably planted about 1837 when Victoria came to the British throne. Some of the world events shown, happened in the same year, so they appear on the same growth ring.

1846 The planet Neptune was discovered

1846 Famine in Ireland

1876 Alexander Bell invents the telephone

1919 Alcock and Brown fly across the Atlantic

1929 Sir Edwin Hubble discovers how to measure the distance of galaxies

1936 TV first broadcast in Britain

Tree Time Lines

Each growth ring in a tree trunk represents one year on an historical time line. The circumference of each ring links together parallel events—that is events that happened at the same time. By looking at parallel events we build up a more complete picture of the past. For example, in the 15th century, when Europeans started to explore westward across the Atlantic Ocean, an Aztec civilisation was flourishing in central America. In 1519, the two cultures met.

When a log canoe was discovered in London in 1987 it was accurately dated from the pattern of the tree rings in the wood. Scientists showed that the canoe was made by the Saxons in AD 950 from an oak tree that was 200 years old when it was felled.

The Age of a Tree

Examine a cross-section from the trunk of a tree. If you know the date that it was felled you can calculate its age by counting the number of rings from the outside edge, in towards the centre. Each ring is one year's growth. The central heartwood can take several years to form.

Decades

Once you have worked out the age of the tree, mark the decades. A decade is a period of 10 years and for some reason a new decade seems to bring change. Ask your parents and grandparents about the 'fifties', 'sixties' and 'seventies'. Record the birth dates of your family on the cross-section and add important world events that have happened during the period of the tree's life.

MORE RECENT EVENTS
The tree from which this cross-section was taken was about 30 years old when it was felled in 1994.
For older people, recent decades are within living memory. What happened in the world in the year that you were born.

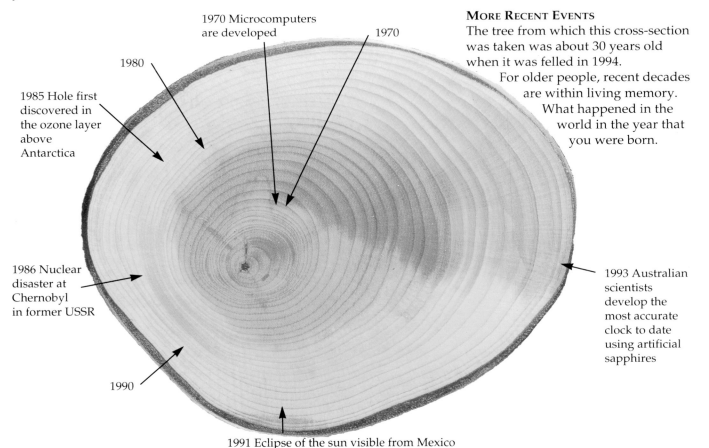

1970 Microcomputers are developed

1970

1980

1985 Hole first discovered in the ozone layer above Antarctica

1986 Nuclear disaster at Chernobyl in former USSR

1990

1991 Eclipse of the sun visible from Mexico

1993 Australian scientists develop the most accurate clock to date using artificial sapphires

Solar Time

You have already seen from your time chart for a day (page 7), just how much of your time is spent sleeping. Our days are governed by day and night, caused by the constant rotation of the Earth on its axis. The passing days and months are counted, recorded and organised into a calendar.

Seasons and Festivals

Early farming civilisations were governed by the **seasons**. Seeds had to be planted at the right time—spring was known as 'growing time'. A good harvest was believed to depend upon the mood of the god of fertility, so rituals and ceremonies developed. A calendar was needed to organise these annual events which later became festivals. Priests arranged the calendar and they became extremely powerful because they could predict the seasons.

The Solar Year

The rhythm of the solar year has always influenced life on Earth and most early civilisations worshipped the sun. Time was very important to the Maya living in central America 1,500 years ago. They observed the natural cycles—the changing seasons, the movement of the stars and the passage of night into day. They accurately calculated the length of one year—just over 365 days.

Mayan Calendars

The Maya used two calendars—the solar year and the sacred round. The solar year had 365 days arranged in 18 months of 20 days each. There were an extra five days of bad luck at the end of each year. The sacred round had a cycle of 20 weeks, each having 13 days. The small wheel turned 20 times, the large 13, completing the 260 day cycle.

THE WHEELS OF THE SACRED ROUND
Bars and dots record numbers: a dot = 1, a bar = 5.

13 revolutions

20 revolutions

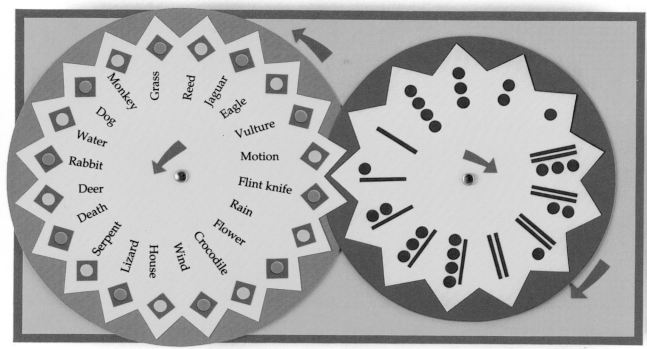

Wheels of Time

The sacred round was made up of two wheels. The smaller wheel was numbered 1-13 and turned clockwise. The larger wheel, bearing the names of the 20 days, turned anti-clockwise. The solar and the sacred calendars ran together making a cycle of 52 years, after which they returned to the starting day.

The Maya were very superstitious. People were named according to the day on which they were born and that day also foretold their destiny. An almanac recorded which days were unlucky. The past and future were the same to the Maya and time had no beginning or end.

Card circles for perpetual calendar

The Cycle of the Seasons

Spring, summer, autumn and winter follow each other in an endless rhythmic cycle. Change in the natural world means renewal and growth.

MAKE A PERPETUAL CALENDAR

To make the calendar you will need five card circles. Write the months of the year around the edge of the largest circle and the numbers 1-31, for the days of the month, around the edge of one of the 12 cm circles.

Cut a window out of the second 12 cm circle to view the date through. Write the days of the week around the edge of the 8 cm circle. Make a pointer on the smallest circle and decorate all the circles with patterns.

Fix all the circles together with a paper fastener. Set the calendar to the right day, date and month, lining them up with the central pointer.

Don't forget to change the date every day.

Perpetual calendar when assembled

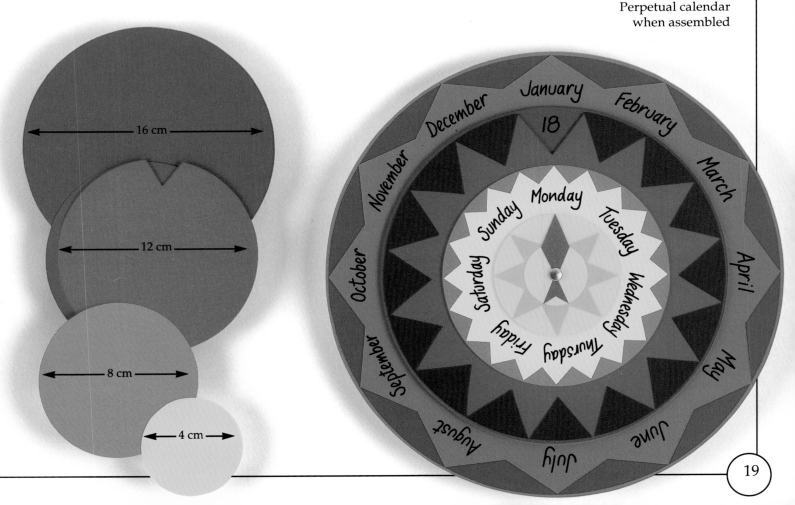

Lunar Time

The **solar year** is the time taken for the Earth to orbit around the sun and the **lunar month**—about 29$\frac{1}{2}$ days—is the time for the moon to travel around the Earth. **Calendar months** are the convenient organisation of days into the **calendar year** which is a quarter of a day shorter than the solar year. To keep the calendar year in step with the solar year, we have a **leap year** once every four years. Until the 16th century, people believed that the Earth was the centre of the universe.

Religious calendars were always organised around the lunar month. The lunar year, about 355 days, is shorter than the solar year. Priests had the task of calculating festival days from the combined calendars. Even today Moslem festivals are arranged to fit in with the lunar calendar.

PHASES OF THE MOON

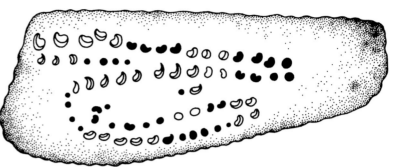

ANCIENT RECORDS
Records of the phases of the moon carved on bone, found in France and approximately 30,000 years old.

Phases of the Moon

As the moon moves around the Earth different parts become sunlit and the moon appears to change shape. We call these apparent changes the **phases of the moon**. Evidence has been found that early civilisations recorded the phases of the moon in picture form. These primitive astronomers would have found it hard to believe that in 1969 astronauts would walk on the moon.

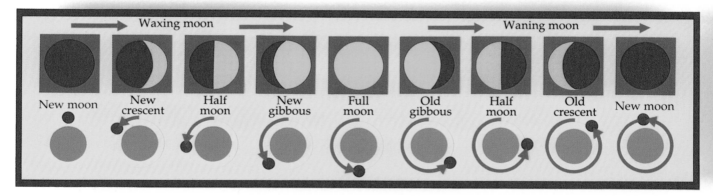

Moonlight

Moonlight is sunlight reflected from the moon's surface. Only one side of the moon is ever visible from Earth. If you look at the full moon through a reflecting telescope you can see mountains and craters on the surface.

Waxing and Waning

The moon, held by gravitational pull, orbits the Earth once every 29$\frac{1}{2}$ days. A lunar month is the time between one new moon and the next. The moon waxes from new moon to full moon, then wanes back to new moon again.

Turning Tides

Twice every day the seas and oceans rise and fall in a rhythmic sequence pulled by the gravitational forces of the sun and the moon. These are the tides.

A spring tide is a very high tide, caused when the sun, moon and Earth are in line. A neap tide is a lower tide which occurs when the moon and sun are pulling at right angles to each other.

We talk about the ebb and flow of the tides. The ecology of the seashore, home and feeding ground to many creatures, exists because of the regularity of the tides.

Changing landscapes

The continual movement of the tides not only erodes our coastlines, but also deposits sand and shingle. The land is being worn away in some places and built up in others. This constant change has been going on since the oceans and land were first formed.

Making a Phantascope

Trace the pattern shown below onto paper. Cut it out and glue it onto a piece of thin card. Allow the glue to dry, then carefully cut out the disc and the viewing slots with a craft knife.

Attach the phantascope disc to a pencil by pushing a drawing pin through the centre point, into the pencil. Stand facing a mirror and slowly turn the phantascope looking at the mirror through the slots. Make sure you turn it in the right direction. Watch the phases of the moon wax and wane.

PATTERN FOR A PHANTASCOPE

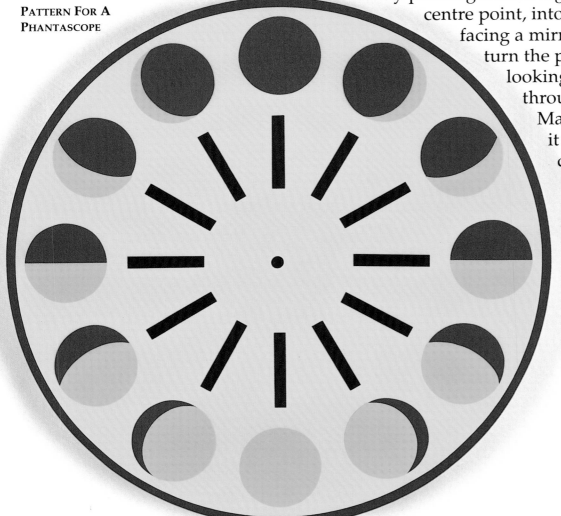

A FLICKER BOOK
The phases of the moon are also shown at the top left corner of each page in this book. Flick through the pages as you would a flicker book and see the moon wax and wane.

Daytime

Daylight

The sun appears to rise in the east each morning. The Earth's rotation makes it seem as if the sun moves across the sky during the day, until it sets in the west at night.

The Earth turns towards the east on an axis between the north and south poles, although we cannot feel it moving. It takes 24 hours, or 1 day, to complete one rotation. At the north and south poles, it moves very slowly, but on the equator it is speeding at 1,700 kilometres an hour!

NORTHERN WINTER AND SOUTHERN SUMMER
The seasons change because the Earth is tilted on its axis and travels in an elliptical orbit round the sun.

The Seasons

The equator divides the Earth into two halves, called the northern and southern **hemispheres**. The Earth rotates on a tilt. We have different seasons because the hemispheres are nearer or further from the sun at different times of year. This is shown in the picture below.

When the northern hemisphere is tilted away from the sun, it has winter. Six months later it is tilted towards the sun and has summer. In the southern hemisphere the opposite happens. In Australia, Christmas is the warmest time of year. Countries on the equator are hot all year round.

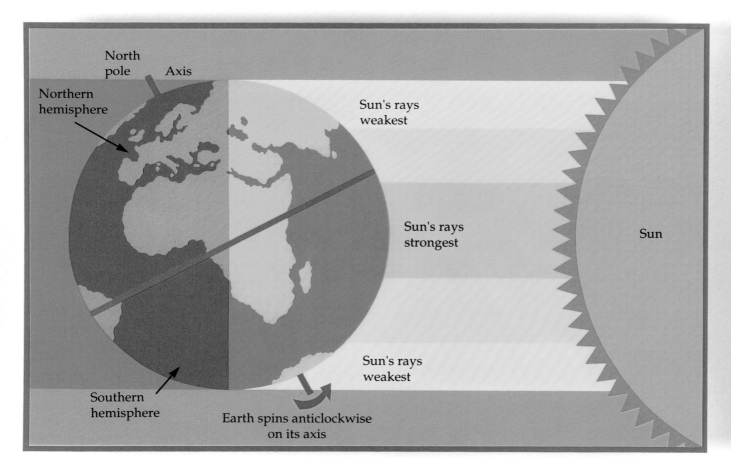

North pole   Axis

Northern hemisphere

Sun's rays weakest

Sun's rays strongest

Sun

Sun's rays weakest

Southern hemisphere

Earth spins anticlockwise on its axis

Shadow Clocks

The sun creates shadows that change in size and direction as the Earth rotates. Shadow clocks and sundials were early 'clocks'. The ancient Egyptians divided both day and night into 12 equal parts. However, the night hours could be longer or shorter than the day hours, depending on the length of the night.

Hours of daylight and darkness vary according to the season. During the winter months, we have long dark nights. At the north and south poles there are times when the sun never rises above the horizon. Only at the **equinoxes** are there 12 hours of day and 12 hours of night for everyone.

Sundials

At about the same time as the Maya were developing their calendar system, the Saxons were using wall-mounted, stone sundials to indicate the time for church services. They divided the day into tides. The words 'noontide' and 'eventide' later became part of the language. A **gnomon** in the centre of the stone dial cast the shadow.

Design a Pocket Sundial

Use a small piece of wood or card as a base. Make a triangular gnomon from card and glue it to the base fixing it along the fold line. Take the sundial outside and mark a shadow at each hour of the day. Make sure you stand in the same place. How accurate is the sundial?

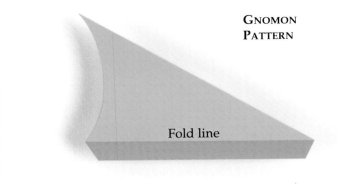

GNOMON PATTERN

Fold line

SHADOW HISTOGRAM

Length of shadow in centimetres

Time of day

Marking Shadows

On a sunny day ask a friend to measure the length of your shadow. Stand in the same place at hourly intervals and record the measurement. What do you notice about your shadow? Make a histogram.

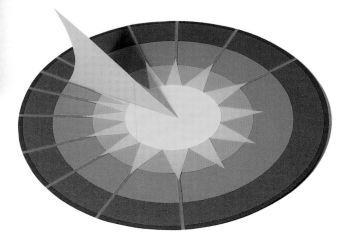

POCKET SUNDIAL

Keeping Time

Nowadays, all through the day and the night, clocks chime the hour or part of the hour. We are constantly made aware of time passing. In schools, lessons begin and end at the same time each day. Railways and buses, aeroplanes and ships, all have organised timetables using 24-hour time. The whole of our lives are organised around the clock.

24–Hour Time
Make a time chart showing 24 hour time. Mark on your chart what you would be doing at each hour.

The 24-Hour Clock
Each day is divided into 24 equal units of time called hours. An hour is an artificial unit of time, measured using an accurate timekeeper like a clock. It is a precise measurement of time.

If using the 24-hour system of time, it is not necessary to use a.m. or p.m. Time is always written using four digits: 01:00 is one o'clock in the morning or 1 a.m.; 13:00 is one o'clock in the afternoon or 1 p.m.

01	02	03	04	05	06	07	08	09	10	11	12	13	14	15	16	17	18	19	20	21	22	23	24
											Midday												Midnight
1	2	3	4	5	6	7	8	9	10	11	12	1	2	3	4	5	6	7	8	9	10	11	12

Morning a.m.   Afternoon p.m.

Time at Sea
Before the invention of a clock that would work on board ship 'watches' were timed using sand-timers (hour glasses). There were 5 four-hour watches every day. The sand-timer ran for 4 hours. In addition, between 4 p.m. and 8 p.m. there were 2 two-hour 'dog' watches.

Eight Bells
Every half hour during each four-hour watch at sea, a bell signalled the passing of time. A 30 minute sand-timer indicated when to ring the bell.

Watches at Sea
Each sailor works for 8 hours, taking two watches per day. The two dog watches count as one. The middle and afternoon watches are worked by the same sailor.

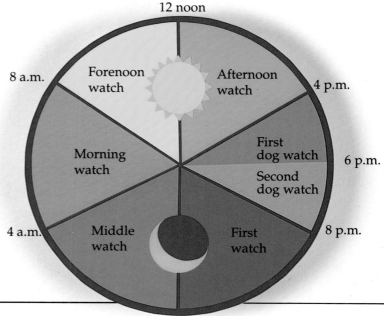

Make a Sand-Timer

A sand-timer, or hour-glass, is simple to make, although it is important to follow some basic rules. The sand inside must be kept perfectly dry. Sieve it first so that all the particles are the same size. The regulator, that is the hole through which the sand flows, can be altered in size.

First find two identical plastic bottles and a piece of card for the regulator, the same diameter as the neck of the bottles. Pierce a hole through the regulator. Do not make it too large at first then you can always alter it later. The larger the hole in the regulator the faster the rate of flow of the sand.

Make sure the bottles are bone dry. Half fill one bottle with dry sieved sand and tape the bottle necks together. Fit the regulator in between. Aim to get your sand-timer to time an exact length of time, like ten minutes or 1 hour. You can adjust the length of time by putting extra sand in the bottles or pouring some away.

Design a stand for your sand-timer. Make a loop from a coat hanger wire. Bend it around the necks of the bottles and twist the ends together. Fold a piece of strong card into a stand as shown here. Push the wire through the front of the stand securing the sand-timer firmly. Now, when the sands of time run out, turn them around and start again!

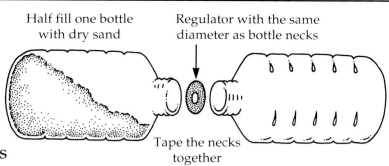

Half fill one bottle with dry sand — Regulator with the same diameter as bottle necks — Tape the necks together

SAND-TIMER AND STAND

Measuring Time

What is the Date?

The Gregorian calendar has been calculated from the year in which Christians believe that Christ was born. Years before Christ's birth are BC, years after are AD— we live in AD 1994. The Jewish religious calendar dates from the creation of the world. The Islamic calendar dates from the flight of Muhammad to Medina.

Dates are important as points of reference in our lives. You remember the date and year of your birth so that you can celebrate your birthday annually.

A century is 100 years. It is an historical measurement of time. We live in the 20th century because of the belief that Christ was born almost 2,000 years ago. A millennium is a thousand years. Soon we will enter a new millennium, the year AD 2000.

Cogs and Wheels

Gear wheels inside a wind-up watch make the hands turn at the right speed. You can make a set of cogs like the ones shown here. You will need coloured card, lollipop sticks and some split pins. Arrange the cogs so that they all mesh together. Which cog turns the fastest and in what direction?

COGS AND WHEELS

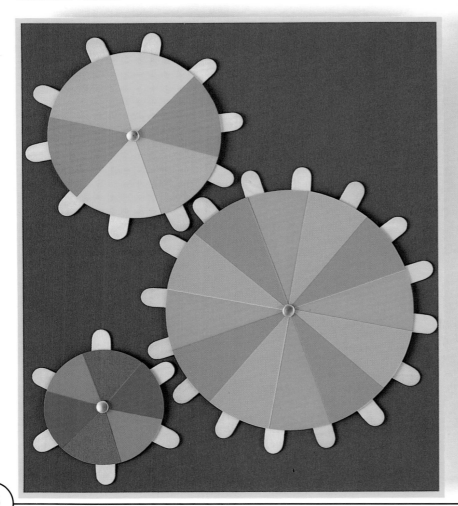

MAKING COGS
Cut out three different size card circles. Cut the lollipop sticks in half and glue them to the card circle. The smaller circle will need fewer sticks. Decorate the circles with patterns. Arrange the cogs on a piece of thick card so that their spokes mesh together. Secure them with split pins.

How to attach sticks

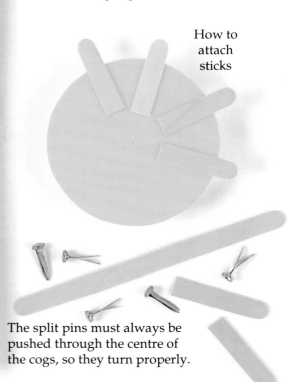

The split pins must always be pushed through the centre of the cogs, so they turn properly.

26

What is the Time?

We use clocks and watches to measure units of time— hours, minutes and seconds. In the 16th century, Galileo noticed the regular swing of the pendulum and for the first time small intervals of time could be measured. If a pendulum is 99.416 cm long each swing is 1 second. The word 'clock' first meant an instrument that strikes.

Natural Time

A whole day, 24 hours, is a natural period of time. A week, an hour, a minute and a second are not. They have been invented by people to help them measure time.

MAKING A TIME MACHINE

Cut a window in the front of the box. Decorate the large cog and position it inside the box so it is visible through the window. Secure it with a split pin.

Slot to turn cogs

Inside of clock showing position of cogs

Attach the small cog so the two cogs mesh together. Glue clock hands to the lower split pin and draw a clock face around them. Decorate the time machine.

Units of Time

Our system of recording time was invented about 5,000 years ago by the Babylonians who used base 60 when calculating large numbers. This means that 60 small units were equal to one large unit.

60 seconds= 1 minute
60 minutes= 1 hour

Make a Time Machine

You can design your own fantastic time machine like the one shown here. Find a strong cardboard box and make a large and small cog as explained opposite. Turn the cogs inside and see time fly.

Travelling Time

Longitude

We divide the surface of the Earth from north to south into segments, like an orange, using imaginary lines called **longitude**. Together the segments equal 360 degrees. The Earth takes 24 hours (1,440 minutes) to rotate on its axis and every degree passes once in front of the sun each day. Every degree travelled is four minutes in time.

LONGITUDE

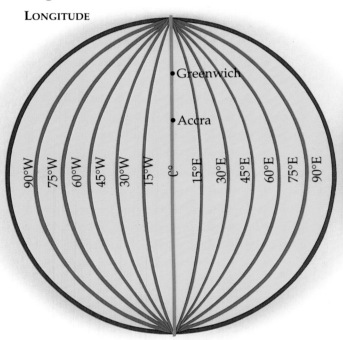

Standard Time

In the past, every place had its own local time which meant that Plymouth was always 16 minutes later than London. When railways were invented timetables became a problem, so all towns in Britain decided to use London time as the **standard time.** Soon after, the world was divided into **time zones**. Each time zone is equivalent to 1 hour and covers 15 degrees of longitude. Moving eastwards 1 hour is added on for every time zone passed through.

Travelling North or South

When travelling along a line of longitude, north or south, you remain in the same time zone for the whole of your journey. The time in Accra, west Africa, is the same as Greenwich in London—they lie on the same line of longitude. This is the Prime Meridian or 0 degrees of longitude. It is known as Greenwich Mean Time or GMT.

TIME ZONES

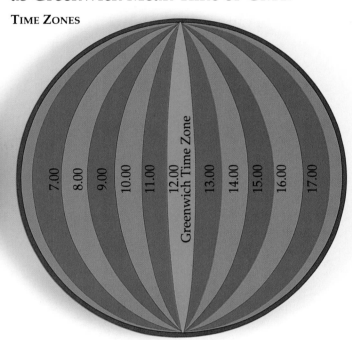

Each time zone is 15° of longitude. The Greenwich time zone is between longitudes 7.5°W and 7.5°E.

Travelling East and West

The longitude of a given place is its distance east or west of the Prime Meridian On board ship sailors must know longitude in order to calculate the exact position of the ship. To calculate longitude it is necessary to know accurately the time at the Prime Meridian. In 1764, John Harrison invented a clock, known as a chronometer, that could keep accurate time at sea.

Time Balls

Before accurate timekeepers were available, sailors on the River Thames knew the correct time at Greenwich at least once a day. A red time ball, raised to the top of a 5 metre mast, was lowered at exactly 1 p.m.

Rolling Balls

In the 16th century Galileo invented the first rolling-ball clock. Other clock makers later refined his ideas using the action of balls rolling down zig-zag slopes to regulate clocks.

Speed

To find out how fast something is travelling you need to know both the time taken and the distance travelled. Using a stop watch you can time speeds to fractions of seconds. To measure the speed at sea, sailors once threw a log overboard which was tied by a rope with knots at equal distances.
They counted the knots that passed over the the side in half a minute.
A knot is one nautical mile per hour.
A nautical mile is $1/60$ of one degree of longitude.

MAKING A ROLLING BALL CLOCK
Make several cardboard slopes as shown here. Fix the slopes onto a piece of board or the side of a cardboard box.

Roll a marble along the slopes making sure the marble rolls from one to the next.

Can you arrange the slopes so that it takes exactly 10 seconds for the marble to roll from top to bottom?

Try using different types of balls like a ping-pong ball or a hard rubber ball. What difference do they make?

Space Time

Looking back in Time

Distances in space are far too great to imagine. Our solar system is a very small part of the galaxy, known to us as the Milky Way. Distance in space is measured in light years. A light year is the distance a ray of light travels in one year—9.5 million million kilometres. A beam of light reflected from Earth will take one second to reach the moon, but 100,000 years to travel across our galaxy.

When we look up into the night sky we see groups of stars called constellations but we are really looking back into time. The Andromeda Galaxy is visible even though it is over 2 million light years away but we see it as it was 2 million years ago. Astronomers there would see the Earth as it was 2 million years ago when the first people made stone tools!

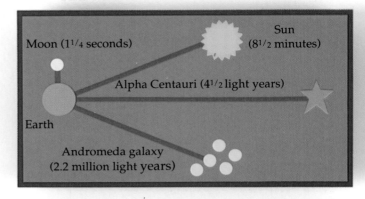

Moon (1¼ seconds) Sun (8½ minutes)

Alpha Centauri (4½ light years)

Earth

Andromeda galaxy (2.2 million light years)

Space Probes

Robotic spacecraft are sent out into space to monitor and photograph the planets and send important data back to Earth. The space probe, Voyager 2, visited Saturn, Uranus and Neptune before passing out of our solar system in 1990. It carries a symbolic message from the people of Earth.

THE SOLAR SYSTEM

Look at the information about our solar system. Venus is similar in size to Earth but a day on Venus lasts as long as 243 days on Earth. The Venusian year, the time it takes to orbit the sun, is only 225 Earth days!

	Mercury	Venus	Earth	Mars	Jupiter	Saturn	Uranus	Neptune	Pluto
Distance from sun (millions of km)	58	108	150	228	778	1,427	2,870	4,497	5,900
Revolutions around sun	88 days*	225 days	365¼ days	687 days	12 years*	29½ years	84 years	165 years	248 years
Rotation period	59 days	243 days	1 day	1 day	10 hours*	10 hours	17 hours	16 hours	6 days
Number of moons	—	—	1	2	16	18 or more	15	8	1

(Astronomers are still discovering new facts about the planets. This data, published in the *National Geographic Magazine*, August 1990, has been rounded to whole numbers.)

*Earth days, hours & years

Postcards from the Planets
Imagine you are taking a holiday on one of the planets. Write a postcard home about your experiences!

Messages through Time
The Voyager 2 space probe carries a message into the future. People often leave messages for future generations to discover. Some have come to us by accident, like the artefacts left by the Egyptians. The pyramids are giant time capsules, giving us insights into a civilisation that existed thousands of years ago.

Time Capsules
Cleopatra's Needle is a granite obelisk, carved in Egypt over 3,500 ago. Since 1878, it has stood on the bank of the River Thames in London. Underneath a remarkable collection of articles is buried—a time capsule for the future. Sealed in large stone jars are every day objects like coins, newspapers and a portrait of Queen Victoria, also a case of cigars and pipes, a razor and some children's toys!

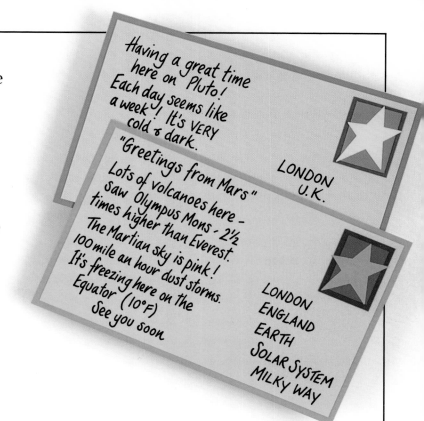

Having a great time here on Pluto! Each day seems like a week! It's VERY cold & dark.

LONDON U.K.

"Greetings from Mars" Lots of volcanoes here - saw Olympus Mons - 2½ times higher than Everest. The Martian sky is pink! 100 mile an hour dust storms. It's freezing here on the Equator (10°F) See you soon

LONDON ENGLAND EARTH SOLAR SYSTEM MILKY WAY

MAKING YOUR OWN TIME CAPSULE
Make your own Time Capsule for the future. Think about who might open it. What articles would best reflect our world today? How best to contain them? Try and include some interesting and unusual items—things that may need saving! Seeds may be useful in the future. Don't forget to write invitations to the opening ceremony.

Invitation to the OPENING of my TIME CAPSULE Sat. 18th April AD 2094 R.S.V.P. (Keep this in a safe place!)

Words & Names

Index

almanac A yearly calendar that gives useful information, such as the phases of the moon and the tides.

ancestors Forefathers from whom you are directly descended.

ancient Very old, dated from a long time ago.

anticlockwise In the opposite direction to the turning of the hands of the clock.

archives A collection of official records holding information about a family or institution.

astronomer A scientist who studies the universe.

chronological order A listing of events in the sequence in which they occurred.

Darwin, Charles (1809-1882) English naturalist who sailed around the world on *The Beagle* (1831-6). Published *The Origin of Species* in 1859.

ecology The relationship between living things and the environment in which they live.

equinoxes The two occasions in the year, March and September, when day and night are of equal length.

Galileo (1564-1642) Italian scientist who laid the foundations for modern science.

generation The time needed for children to grow up and take the place of their parents, usually about 35 years in humans. A group of people, of similar age, sharing similar attitudes and experiences.

germination The process by which a seed starts to grow.

gnomon A fixed pointer that projects a shadow on to a sundial.

Gregorian calendar The calendar system that divides the year into 365 days. Introduced in 1582, by Pope Gregory XIII, to replace the existing Julian calendar. Still in use today.

Harrison, John (1692-1776) Also known as 'Longitude Harrison', inventor of the first accurate ship's chronometer.

hibernate To pass the winter in a state of dormancy by the slowing down of the body's metabolism.

leap year A calendar year of 366 days occurring every four years. Always in a year in which the digits are divisible by four. February 29th is the extra leap day.

memorabilia Things or events that are memorable.

metamorphosis A complete change of appearance, as when a caterpillar becomes a butterfly.

radioactive Material that decays to another substance on a precise time basis. The age of rock is estimated from the amount of radioactive carbon it contains—a process known as radiocarbon dating.

synchronise Events that happen in unison, or at the same time.

Voyager 2 The second of two space probes launched by the USA in 1977 to explore the outer solar system. It carries a record disc called *Sounds of Earth* and was still sending back signals to Earth in 1993 after a 4.43 billion mile journey.